180 DEVOTIONS
FOR THE SCHOOL YEAR

MAKE it COUNT

SUE CHRISTIAN

Abingdon Press / *Nashville*

180 Devotions for the School Year

Copyright © 2012 by Abingdon Press

This book is printed on acid-free paper.

ISBN 978-1-4267-4462-4

Scripture quotations are from the Common English Bible. Copyright © 2011 by the Common English Bible. All rights reserved. Used by permission. www.CommonEnglishBible.com

12 13 14 15 16 17 18 19 20 21—10 9 8 7 6 5 4 3 2 1

MANUFACTURED IN THE UNITED STATES OF AMERICA

1.80

A NEW SCHOOL YEAR IS HERE. THINK OF IT AS A BLANK SLATE WITH INFINITE POSSIBILITIES. WHEN GOD CREATED THE EARTH, IT WAS A BLANK SLATE TOO. AS YOU TAKE EACH DAY OF YOUR NEW SCHOOL YEAR, INCLUDE GOD TO HELP FORM IT.

When God began to create the heavens and the earth—the earth was without shape or form.

—Genesis 1:1-2

1 7 9

EACHDAY, AS YOU TURN A PAGE IN THIS
BOOK, YOU WILL BE ABLE TO READ A
VERSE FROM SCRIPTURE. LET'S BEGIN
THIS NEW SCHOOL YEAR WITH GOD!

Every scripture is inspired by God and is
useful for teaching, for showing mistakes, for
correcting, and for training character, so that
the person who belongs to God can be
equipped to do everything that is good.

—2 Timothy 3:16-17

USE THE MIND GOD GAVE YOU.

WORK HARD AT SCHOOL THIS NEW YEAR
AND GET THE BEST GRADES POSSIBLE.
GRADES ARE CURRENCY TO GET YOU
INTO THE CLASSES AND SCHOOLS YOU
WANT IN THE FUTURE.

God didn't give us a spirit that is timid but one

that is powerful, loving, and self-controlled.

—2 Timothy 1:7

177

IN GENESIS 3:3 GOD TOLD ADAM AND EVE NOT TO EAT THE FRUIT FROM A CERTAIN TREE, BUT THEY COULD NOT RESIST. PEER PRESSURE IS A TOUGH THING. THERE WILL BE MANY DECISIONS YOU HAVE TO MAKE THAT WILL AFFECT YOU EVERY DAY. LISTEN TO THE HOLY SPIRIT IF YOU ARE FEELING CONFLICT OR CONFUSION ABOUT WHAT YOU SHOULD DO.

The woman saw that the tree was beautiful with delicious food and that the tree would provide wisdom, so she took some of its fruit and ate it, and also gave some to her husband, who was with her, and he ate it.

—*Genesis 3:6*

176

IDOLS CAN BE FOOTBALL, CELL PHONES, TV, FRIENDS, OR WHATEVER YOU FEEL YOU CAN'T LIVE WITHOUT. REMEMBER TO ALWAYS KEEP GOD FIRST. THEN ROUND UP A GROUP OF FRIENDS AND GO TO A FOOTBALL GAME.

I am the LORD;

that is my name;

I don't hand out my glory to others

or my praise to idols.

—Isaiah 42:8

175

JESUS, WHO IS THE SON OF GOD, NEEDED TO PRAY. AFTER HE PRAYED, HE ACCEPTED WHAT GOD WANTED FOR HIM. IF JESUS HAD TO PRAY, THINK HOW MUCH MORE WE DO!

Then he went a short distance farther and fell on his face and prayed, "My Father, if it's possible, take this cup of suffering away from me. However—not what I want but what you want."

—Matthew 26:39

FAITH IS THE MOST IMPORTANT THING IN THE CHRISTIAN WALK. YOU NEED TO HAVE FAITH THAT THERE IS A GOD AND THAT HE LOVES YOU AND CARES ABOUT YOU WHETHER YOU ARE HOME, AT SCHOOL, OR WITH YOUR FRIENDS.

It's impossible to please God without faith because the one who draws near to God must believe that he exists and that he rewards people who try to find him.

—Hebrews 11:6

173

PRAY TO THE LORD AND ASK HIM FOR GUIDANCE IN ALL AREAS OF YOUR LIFE. HE WILL BE WITH YOU AS YOU PREPARE FOR WHAT YOU HAVE TO DO AND THEN WHEN YOU ARE DOING IT. MOSES WAS NOT A SPEAKER, BUT YET WITH GOD HE WAS ABLE TO SPEAK IN FRONT OF THE PHARAOH. LEAN ON GOD WHEN YOU THINK YOU CAN'T DO SOMETHING YOU HAVE BEEN ASKED TO DO.

But Moses said to the LORD, "My Lord, I've never been able to speak well. . . ."

Then the LORD said to him, "Who gives people the ability to speak? . . . Isn't it I, the LORD? Now go! I'll help you speak, and I'll teach you what you should say."

—Exodus 4:10a, 11a, c, 12

THE TEN COMMANDMENTS LIST TEN
THINGS GOD SAYS YOU SHOULD NEVER DO.
YOU CAN FIND THEM IN EXODUS 20:2-17.
THINK ABOUT THE FIRST FIVE TODAY.

1. *Worship only God.*

2. *Do not worship idols (that is, stars, sports, money, and things. Enjoy them, but put them in their proper place).*

3. *Don't use the Lord's name as if it were of no significance.*

4. *Remember the Sabbath and keep it holy.*

5. *Honor your mother and father.*

　　　　　—Exodus 20:2-12 (author's condensation)

REMEMBER, NO ONE IS PERFECT BUT
GOD. HE IS THE ONE WHO SEES INTO
YOUR HEART AND HAS MERCY. HE KNOWS
YOUR HEART'S INTENTIONS.

6. *Do not kill.*

7. *Do not commit adultery.*

8. *Do not steal.*

9. *Do not testify falsely against your neighbors (or persons at school)*

10. *Do not desire what your neighbor or friend has.*

—Exodus 20:13-17 (author's condensation)

170

THIS CAN BE A HARD ONE TO DO. OUR HUMAN NATURE WANTS TO GET EVEN, BUT GOD TELLS US TO LOVE OUR ENEMIES. BY LOVING OUR ENEMIES, GOD MEANS FOR US TO NOT RETALIATE. GET AWAY FROM THE SITUATION, AND THEN TURN YOUR MIND FROM REVENGE TO PRAYER.

"But I say to you, love your enemies and pray for those who harass you."

—Matthew 5:44

DO YOU REALLY WANT TO KNOW GOD? YOU MAY FEEL YOU ARE "NOT DOING IT RIGHT," BUT GOD KNOWS YOUR HEART AND YOUR INTENTIONS. KEEP BEING HONEST WITH HIM IN YOUR PRAYERS, AND HE WILL HEAR YOU.

You will seek the LORD your God

from there, and you will find him if

you seek him with all your heart

and with all your being.

—Deuteronomy 4:29

EVERYONE LOVES TO GET PRAISE AND RESPECT. WHEN YOU DO SOMETHING FOR SOMEONE AND IT GOES UNNOTICED, DON'T TELL ANYONE. GOD WILL KNOW, AND YOU WILL BE AMAZED, IF YOU KEEP YOUR EYES OPEN, HOW HE WILL REWARD YOU.

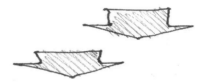

"Whenever you give to the poor, don't blow your trumpet as the hypocrites do in the synagogues and in the streets so that they may get praise from people. I assure you, that's the only reward they'll get."

—Matthew 6:2

WHEN WE APPRECIATE WHAT OTHERS DO AND TELL THEM, WE SHOW OUR MATURITY AND WISDOM. BY THANKING OR COMPLIMENTING PERSONS, WE AFFIRM WHO THEY ARE.

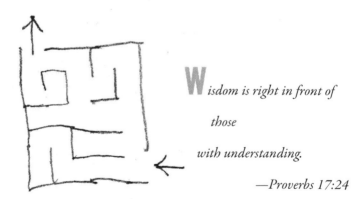

Wisdom is right in front of

those

with understanding.

—Proverbs 17:24

IN SCHOOL THERE IS A LOT OF TALK ABOUT OTHERS, AND SOME OF IT CAN BE UNKIND. BE CAREFUL WITH WHAT YOU HEAR ABOUT SOMEONE ELSE. GOSSIP CAN BE VERY DANGEROUS.

A solitary witness against someone in any crime, wrongdoing, or in any sort of misdeed that might be done is not sufficient. The decision must stand by two or three witnesses.

—Deuteronomy 19:15

165

DO YOU EVER SEE ANY "GOLIATHS" AT SCHOOL? PEOPLE MAY TRY TO DISCOURAGE YOU OR MAKE FUN OF YOU FOR TAKING THEM ON, BUT BY DOING WHAT IS RIGHT YOU WILL BE PLEASING GOD, WHO MATTERS THE MOST.

↓   ↓   ↙

Goliath was a Philistine who was a giant of a man over nine feet tall. David was a shepherd who told the giant he had God with him and met him in battle. Then with five stones and a sling, he kills Goliath!

—1 Samuel 17:32-57 (author's condensation)

FRIENDSHIP IS IMPORTANT. FEELING GOD'S LOVE MEANS YOU WILL CARE ABOUT YOUR FRIENDS. MAKE SURE YOU TREAT THEM AS YOU WOULD LIKE TO BE TREATED.

"This is my commandment: love each other just as I have loved you. No one has greater love than to give up one's life for one's friends."

—John 15:12-14

163

A LITTLE SIN CAN GROW UNTIL IT CAN BE YOUR DOWNFALL. CONFESS YOUR SINS AND ASK GOD FOR STRENGTH TO RESIST TEMPTATION. SOLOMON WAS THE WISEST KING EVER UNTIL HE LET SIN CREEP INTO HIS HEART LITTLE BY LITTLE, ALWAYS RATIONALIZING TO HIMSELF THAT IT WAS OK. DON'T LET THIS HAPPEN TO YOU.

The LORD grew angry with Solomon, because his heart had turned away from being with the LORD, the God of Israel, who had appeared to him twice.

—*1 Kings 11:9*

GOD MAY HAVE PLACED YOU IN YOUR SCHOOL, IN YOUR JOB, OR WITH YOUR FRIENDS TO BE A WITNESS FOR HIM. IT IS NOT ALWAYS AN EASY THING TO DO BUT, JUST AS GOD PUT ESTHER WITH KING AHASUERUS'S ROYAL FAMILY, GOD MAY HAVE PUT YOU WITH A PARTICULAR PERSON TO HELP HIM OR HER AT THIS TIME.

"In fact, if you don't speak up at this very important time, relief and rescue will appear for the Jews from another place, but you and your family will die. But who knows? Maybe it was for a moment like this that you came to be part of the royal family."

—Esther 4:14

161

DISCIPLINE IS NOT FUN, AND GOING THROUGH IT
YOU MAY NOT UNDERSTAND WHY. AS YOU GROW
AND LEARN FROM IT, YOU WILL BUILD A STRONG
FOUNDATION FOR YOURSELF FOR LATER.

No discipline is fun while it lasts, but it seems painful at the

time. Later, however, it yields the peaceful fruit of righteousness

for those who have been trained by it.

—Hebrews 12:11

WHEN YOU GO TO BED, TAKE COMFORT IN REALIZING THAT GOD DOESN'T SLEEP AND HE IS WITH YOU AT ALL TIMES. I USED TO TELL MY DAUGHTER TO THINK OF GOD'S GIANT HAND HOLDING HER AS SHE SLEPT AND TO REST IN HIM.

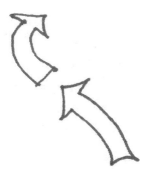

I lie down, sleep, and wake up

because the LORD helps me.

—Psalm 3:5

159

A VERY IMPORTANT VERSE IN THE BIBLE IS JOHN 3:16. HAVE YOU TOLD JESUS THAT YOU ARE A SINNER AND BELIEVE HE DIED FOR YOU? IF YOU HAVEN'T, FIND A QUIET PLACE AND TELL JESUS THAT YOU KNOW YOU ARE A SINNER AND THAT YOU WANT HIM TO BE LORD OVER YOUR LIFE. TELL SOMEONE WHO CAN HELP YOU WITH THE QUESTIONS YOU WILL HAVE. I PROMISE HE OR SHE WILL BE HAPPY FOR YOU!

"God so loved the world that he gave his only Son, so that everyone who believes in him won't perish but will have eternal life."

—John 3:16

158

THIS IS THE NEXT VERSE AFTER JOHN 3:16. GOD IS A GOD OF LOVE. HE HAD TO SACRIFICE HIS OWN SON SO THAT WE COULD COME LIVE WITH HIM IN ETERNITY. EACH PERSON MUST MAKE HIS OR HER OWN DECISION WHERE TO STAND WITH JESUS.

"God didn't send his Son into the world to judge the world, but that the world might be saved through him. Whoever believes in him isn't judged; whoever doesn't believe in him is already judged, because they don't believe in the name of God's only Son."

—*John 3:17*

WHEN YOU LOOK UP ON A CLEAR, DARK NIGHT, YOU
SEE SO MANY STARS. IT IS AMAZING THAT GOD MADE
EACH ONE. HOW BEAUTIFUL THEY ARE. THE GOD
WHO MADE THE STARS MADE YOU. HE LOVES YOU
MORE THAN ANYTHING HE MADE ON THIS EARTH.

> When I look up at your skies,
>   at what your fingers made—
>   the moon and the stars
>   that you set firmly in place—
>   what are human beings
>   that you think about them . . . ?
> You've made them only slightly
>   less than divine,
>   crowning them with glory and grandeur.
>
> —Psalm 8:3-4a, 5

TAKE COMFORT IN THE FACT THAT THE LORD IS ALWAYS WITH YOU AT SCHOOL, HOME, AND WORK. YOU ALWAYS HAVE SOMEONE TO TALK TO IN THE PRIVATE RECESSES OF YOUR MIND.

I always put the LORD in front of me;

I will not stumble

because he is on my right side.

—Psalm 16:8

155

AUTUMN IS HERE. WHAT AN AMAZING SEASON GOD HAS DESIGNED. WHEN YOU SEE THE LEAVES CHANGE, EAT A SLICE OF PUMPKIN BREAD, OR SIP APPLE CIDER, THANK HIM!

They don't say in their hearts,

Let's fear the LORD our God,

who provides rain in autumn and spring

and who assures us of a harvest

in its season.

—*Jeremiah 5:24*

154

TAKE SOME TIME TODAY TO RUN THROUGH SOME LEAVES, SING IN THE SHOWER, DO A CARTWHEEL, OR WHATEVER MAKES YOU SMILE. GOD LOVES IT WHEN YOU ENJOY EACH MOMENT.

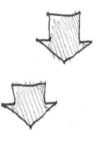

Sing to him a new song!

Play your best with joyful shouts!

—Psalm 33:3

153

GOD GAVE YOU YOUR LIFE. YOU ARE THE ONLY ONE WHO HAS LIVED YOUR LIFE EACH DAY THAT HAS LED EACH STEP OF THE WAY. HE WILL BE WITH YOU ON YOUR NEXT BREATH AND FOR THE REST OF YOUR LIFE.

Life and kindness you gave me,

and you oversaw and

preserved my breath.

—*Job 10:12*

152

YOU WILL HAVE MANY BIG AND LITTLE DECISIONS TO MAKE AS YOU GROW OLDER. IF YOU TAKE TIME WITH GOD NOW, HE WILL GUIDE YOU IN YOUR PATHS FOR THE FUTURE.

Where are the ones who honor the LORD?

God will teach them which path to take.

They will live a good life,

and their descendants

will possess the land.

—Psalm 25:12-13

GOD IS A GOD OF HOPE. YOU MAY NOT SEE A WAY OUT OF YOUR PRESENT SITUATION, BUT TELL GOD ABOUT IT AND HAVE HOPE THAT GOD WILL HELP YOU THROUGH WHAT YOU ARE DEALING WITH.

Hope in the LORD!

Be strong! Let your heart

take courage!

Hope in the LORD!

—*Psalm 27:14*

150

NO MATTER WHAT PART OF THE COUNTRY YOU
ARE IN, GOD SURROUNDS YOU WITH HIS
CREATIONS. REST YOUR EYE ON WHAT HE
MADE—THE SKY, CLOUDS, STARS, MOUNTAINS,
SAND, OR TREES—AND KNOW THAT THE ONE WHO
CREATED THEM CREATED YOU AND LOVES YOU.

I raise my eyes toward the mountains.

Where will my help come from?

My help comes from the LORD,

the maker of heaven and earth.

God won't let your foot slip.

Your protector won't fall asleep

on the job.

—*Psalm 121:1-3*

149

DON'T TRY TO FIND PEACE WITH EARTHLY THINGS. WE THINK THAT IF WE GET A NEW CAR, CLOTHES, SPORTS EQUIPMENT, OR SUCH, WE WILL ATTAIN HAPPINESS AND PEACE. ONCE YOU GET THOSE THINGS, A NEW DESIGN WILL COME OUT! REMEMBER THAT TO FIND TRUE PEACE, YOU NEED TO BE FILLED WITH THE HOLY SPIRIT AND SEEK GOD. GOD WANTS YOU TO HAVE "FUN TOYS," BUT DON'T LOOK AT THEM TO BRING YOU PEACE; ONLY GOD CAN DO THAT.

Let the LORD bless his people with peace!

—Psalm 29:11b

148

TAKE TIME TO LOOK AT THE MORNING SUNRISE AND THE EVENING SUNSET. LOOK AT THE TREES AS THEY CHANGE WITH THE SEASONS. REFLECT ON THE MAKER OF THESE AND HIS HANDIWORK.

Heaven is declaring God's glory;

the sky is proclaiming his

handiwork.

—Psalm 19:1

147

YOU CAN ALWAYS PRAY BY YOURSELF IN YOUR
ROOM AS YOU ARE TOLD TO DO IN MATTHEW 6:6.
YOU CAN ALSO PRAY IN PRIVATE IN YOUR HEAD AT
SCHOOL, AT A FRIEND'S HOUSE, OR AT WORK.

*"But when you pray, go to your room, shut the door, and
pray to your Father who is present in that secret place. Your
Father who sees what you do in secret will reward you."*

—Matthew 6:6

WHEN YOU ACT OUT WITHOUT THINKING, YOU COULD DO OR SAY SOMETHING YOU WILL REGRET. THIS CAN HAPPEN WITH YOUR PARENTS, AS YOU ARE COMING FROM DIFFERENT VIEWS. KEEP YOUR WORDS AND ACTIONS UNDER CONTROL, AND THE SITUATION WILL BE FIXED MUCH MORE QUICKLY.

Let go of anger and

leave rage behind!

Don't get upset—

it will only lead to evil.

—Psalm 37:8

145

WE ALWAYS WANT THINGS TO BE FAIR IN LIFE. WE ARE ALL SINNERS AND THEREFORE NEED TO BE FORGIVEN BY OUR HEAVENLY FATHER. HOW CAN A RIGHTEOUS GOD FORGIVE YOUR SINS IF YOU WILL NOT FORGIVE THE SINS OF OTHERS? EACH DAY WAKE UP AND TRY TO RELEASE THE UNFORGIVENESS IN YOUR HEART.

"If you forgive others their sins, your heavenly Father will also forgive you. But if you don't forgive others, neither will your Father forgive your sins."

—*Matthew 6:14-15*

144

THE LORD ASKS US TO BE FLEXIBLE IN OUR SCHEDULES SO WE CAN DO WHAT HE MIGHT ASK US TO DO. TRY TO ADAPT TO CHANGES IN PLANS AND SEE WHAT BLESSINGS CAN COME OUT OF IT. I AM SURE ABRAHAM THOUGHT HE WOULD LIVE IN EGYPT ALL HIS LIFE, BUT GOD DID WONDERS WITH HIM AS HE OBEYED GOD AND WANDERED IN THE DESERT FOR FORTY YEARS.

The LORD said to Abram, "Leave your land, your family, and your father's household for the land that I will show you. I will make of you a great nation and will bless you."

—Genesis 12:1-2

143

THERE IS SO MUCH GOING ON IN OUR
WORLD, COUNTRY, STATE, TOWN, AND
SCHOOL. NEVER FORGET THAT GOD IS IN
CONTROL. RUN TO HIM IN PRAYER WHEN
YOU FEEL OVERWHELMED.

God is our refuge and strength,

a help always near

in times of great trouble.

—Psalm 46:1

TODAY DO SOMETHING DIFFERENT! TAKE TIME TO MAKE A HAPPY MEMORY. GOD WANTS YOU TO SHOUT FOR JOY AND WEAR A BIG SMILE. TODAY IS A GIFT FOR YOU FROM GOD; TAKE SOME TIME TO BE GOOD TO YOURSELF!

Clap your hands, all you people!

Shout joyfully to God

with a joyous shout!

—Psalm 47:1

141

WE WERE ALL CHILDREN ONCE AND WILL ALL BE
OLD AT SOME TIME. THE BIBLE IS VERY CLEAR ON
HOW WE ARE TO TREAT PEOPLE YOUNGER AND
OLDER THAN WE ARE—WITH RESPECT. GO OUT OF
YOUR WAY FOR THE OLDER AND YOUNGER
GENERATIONS, AND YOU WILL BE BLESSED IN THE
PROCESS TOO!

Don't correct an older man but encourage
him like he's your father; treat younger men
like your brothers, treat older women like
your mother, and treat younger women like
your sisters with appropriate respect.

—1 Timothy 5:1-2

FRIENDSHIP IS SUCH A VALUABLE THING. LOOK AROUND YOUR SCHOOL AND SEE IF THERE IS A PERSON YOU CAN BECOME FRIENDS WITH WHO NEEDS SOMEONE TO TAKE THE TIME TO NOTICE HIM OR HER. MAYBE YOU CAN BEFRIEND THIS PERSON. YOU MAY BE GETTING TO KNOW A VERY SPECIAL PERSON AND MAKING A BIG DIFFERENCE IN SOMEONE'S LIFE.

Keep loving each other like family. Don't neglect to open up your homes to guests, because by doing this some have been hosts to angels without knowing it.

—Hebrews 13:1-2

139

BE CAREFUL ABOUT HOW YOU USE THE NAME OF THE LORD. THINK OF HOW YOU WOULD WATCH YOUR WORDS IF YOU WERE SPEAKING TO YOUR FAVORITE MOVIE STAR OR SPORTS STAR. GOD IS HOLY AND PERFECT, SO NEVER FORGET THAT. TREAT HIM CORRECTLY.

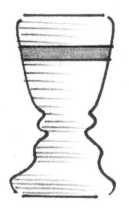

You must not make
my holy name impure.

—*Leviticus 22:32*

YOUR TEACHERS HAVE GONE TO SCHOOL TO BE ABLE TO TEACH YOU WHAT YOU NEED TO LEARN. GOD TELLS US TO RESPECT PEOPLE IN AUTHORITY. LISTEN AND LEARN WHAT YOUR TEACHERS ARE TEACHING YOU.

Because the Teacher was wise, he constantly taught the people knowledge. He listened and investigated.

—*Ecclesiastes 12:9*

137

THE ONLY WAY TO TRULY THIRST FOR GOD IS TO SPEND TIME GETTING TO KNOW HIM. SPEND TIME WITH HIM IN HIS LOVE STORY TO YOU, THE BIBLE. MAKE SURE YOU HAVE A TRANSLATION THAT MAKES SENSE TO YOU. IF YOU DON'T, ASK YOUR PARENTS OR PASTOR TO HELP YOU SELECT ONE.

God! My God! It's you—

I search for you!

My whole being thirsts for you!

—*Psalm 63:1*

LOVE IS CERTAINLY A THEME THROUGHOUT THE BIBLE. IT MERITS BEING REPEATED! "LOVE EACH OTHER" MEANS BE RESPECTFUL, PATIENT, AND KIND TO EACH OTHER. PRAYERFULLY, PEOPLE ARE BEING KIND TO YOU! REMEMBER, GOD LOVES YOU!

This is the message that you heard from the beginning: love each other.

—*1 John 3:11*

135

DECISIONS YOU MAKE TODAY CAN CHANGE YOUR LIFE TOMORROW. BE OBEDIENT TO THE WORD OF GOD AND STAY AWAY FROM PEOPLE OR THINGS THAT COULD CHANGE THE COURSE OF YOUR LIFE IN A NEGATIVE WAY.

The news of your obedience has reached everybody,

so I'm happy for you. But I want you to be wise

about what's good, and innocent about what's evil.

—*Romans 16:19*

WE ALL HAVE SPECIAL GIFTS THAT GOD HAS GIVEN US. HE WANTS US TO USE THEM. BE CAREFUL NOT TO THINK TOO HIGHLY OF YOURSELF IF YOU ARE A SCHOLAR, MUSICIAN, OR ATHLETE. REMEMBER, THE ONLY REASON YOU HAVE THOSE GIFTS IS THAT GOD GAVE THEM TO YOU. USE THEM TO THE FULLEST, BUT GIVE CREDIT FOR THEM TO GOD, NOT YOURSELF.

Pride comes before disaster,

and arrogance before a fall.

—*Proverbs 16:18*

133

TRY THIS TODAY OR TOMORROW MORNING AND SEE WHAT IT BRINGS. TELL GOD WHAT YOUR DAY IS LIKE AND ASK HIM TO BLESS IT. LOOK FOR ALL THE SMALL AND BIG BLESSINGS HE BRINGS. REMEMBER, EVEN HEARING A BIRD SING IS A BLESSING!

LORD, in the morning you hear my voice.

In the morning I lay it all out before you.

Then I wait expectantly.

—Psalm 5:3

IT IS EASY TO FOCUS ON THE NEGATIVE. JUST FOR TODAY, TRY TO FOCUS ON THE GOOD THINGS THAT ARE IN YOUR LIFE. GOD HAS GIVEN YOU MANY BLESSINGS. TAKE THE TIME TO LOOK FOR THEM. START TODAY!

Let my whole being bless the LORD!

Let everything inside me

bless his holy name!

—Psalm 103:1

131

IF YOU FEEL FAR AWAY FROM GOD, KEEP ON SEARCHING. DON'T BE AFRAID TO ASK FOR HELP FROM YOUR YOUTH PASTOR OR PARENTS. GOD WANTS YOU TO BE TRANSPARENT. THERE ARE ALWAYS QUESTIONS ABOUT WHY GOD ALLOWS WHAT HE DOES. AS YOU SEEK HIM WITH THE HELP OF OTHERS, YOU WILL DRAW CLOSER TO HIM.

Pursue the LORD and his strength;

seek his face always!

—Psalm 105:4

ISN'T IT A GREAT THOUGHT THAT GOD LOVES US EVEN WHEN WE MESS UP? HE ALWAYS GIVES US A NEW DAY AND A FRESH START. RENEW YOURSELF EVERY MORNING WITH GOD.

Certainly the faithful love

of the LORD hasn't ended;

certainly God's compassion

isn't through!

They are renewed every morning.

Great is your faithfulness.

—*Lamentations 3:22-23*

129

REMEMBER, SOMEONE WILL ALWAYS

HAVE MORE THAN YOU AND SOMEONE
WILL ALWAYS HAVE LESS. ENJOY WHAT
YOU HAVE AND DON'T WASTE TIME OR
ENERGY CHASING THE WIND OF DESIRE.

It's better to enjoy what's at hand than to have an

insatiable appetite. This too is pointless, just wind chasing.

—*Ecclesiastes 6:9*

PEOPLE TODAY PUT SO MUCH EMPHASIS ON APPEARANCE, BUT THE LORD LOOKS INTO A PERSON'S HEART. WHEN GOD LOOKS PAST YOUR CLOTHES, WHAT DOES HE SEE?

But the LORD said to Samuel, "Have no regard for his appearance or stature, because I haven't selected him. God doesn't look at things like humans do. Humans see only what is visible to the eyes, but the LORD sees into the heart."

—1 Samuel 16:7

127

GOD FORGIVES YOU COMPLETELY. WHEN YOU ASK FOR FORGIVENESS, GOD WILL NEVER BRING THE INCIDENT BACK TO HIS MIND. HE DOESN'T KEEP TRACK OF OUR SINS. NEITHER SHOULD YOU.

Let my whole being bless the LORD
and never forget all his good deeds:
how God forgives all your sins.

—Psalm 103:2-3

EVEN IF YOU KNOW A PERSON IS DOING
SOMETHING WRONG, BE CAREFUL OF YOUR WORDS.
PROUD PEOPLE DO NOT LIKE TO BE CORRECTED,
AND YOU MAY END UP IN AN ARGUMENT.
SOMETIMES IT IS BETTER TO KEEP YOUR COMMENTS
TO YOURSELF UNLESS THAT PERSON IS HURTING
YOU.

Whoever instructs the cynic

gets insulted;

whoever corrects the wicked gets hurt.

Don't correct the impudent,

or they will hate you;

correct the wise,

and they will love you.

—*Proverbs 9:7-8*

125

IT SOUNDS SCARY TO ASK GOD TO EXAMINE
YOU, BUT HE IS A LOVING GOD WHO WANTS
ONLY THE BEST FOR YOU. IF THERE IS ANYTHING
GOD SHOULD NUDGE YOU TO CHANGE, PRAY
FOR HIM TO DO THAT SO YOU WILL BE ON A PATH
OF RIGHTEOUSNESS.

Examine me, God! Look at my heart!

Put me to the test!

Know my anxious thoughts!

Look to see if there is any idolatrous

way in me,

then lead me on the eternal path!

—*Psalm 139:23-24*

THINK ABOUT IT: GOD WANTED YOU SO MUCH HE CREATED YOU. THINK ABOUT THE FACT THAT YOU ARE VERY SPECIAL TO A GOD WHO ALSO CREATED MOUNT EVEREST AND ALL THE STARS IN THE SKY. YET YOU ARE MORE IMPORTANT THAN ANY OF THESE.

"Before I created you in the womb

I knew you;

before you were born I set you apart."

—Jeremiah 1:5-6

123

WHEN YOU TAKE TIME TO THINK OF ALL GOD HAS CREATED AND DONE, YOU WILL SIT IN AWE OF HIM. HE IS THE GREAT PHYSICIAN, COMFORTER, KING OF KINGS, MIGHTY FORTRESS, REDEEMER, FATHER, FRIEND, AND SO MUCH MORE. HE IS AVAILABLE TO YOU EVERY DAY.

The LORD is great

and so worthy of praise!

God's greatness can't be grasped.

—Psalm 145:3

IT IS EASY TO CALL TO GOD ONLY WHEN YOU NEED HELP AND THEN WHEN THE CRISIS IS OVER FORGET ABOUT HIM. THINK HOW THIS WOULD FEEL TO YOU AND TAKE TIME TO DEEPEN YOUR RELATIONSHIP WITH GOD. YOU WILL NEVER REGRET IT!

The LORD is close to everyone

who calls out to him,

to all who call out to him sincerely.

—*Psalm 145:18*

121

WE DO NOT HAVE GOD'S MIND, SO WE TRUST THAT HE KNOWS WHAT IS BEST FOR US. GOD IS PERFECT. NO ONE ON EARTH CAN SHARE THAT CLAIM. TRUST HIM IN YOUR LIFE.

Trust in the LORD with all your heart;

don't rely on your own intelligence.

Know him in all your paths,

and he will keep your ways straight.

—*Proverbs 3:5-6*

120

THANKSGIVING IS A WONDERFUL HOLIDAY.

IT IS A TIME WHEN YOU HAVE A FEW DAYS OFF FROM SCHOOL AND WILL BE WITH FAMILY, FRIENDS, OR RELATIVES. YOU SHOULD BE THANKFUL FOR ALL YOU HAVE. DON'T FORGET TO THANK GOD FOR ALL HE HAS GIVEN YOU.

Give thanks in every situation because this is God's will for you in Christ Jesus.

—1 Thessalonians 5:18

119

WATCH WHAT YOU READ, WHAT MUSIC YOU LISTEN TO, AND WHAT MOVIES YOU WATCH. IF YOU FILL YOUR MIND WITH JUNK, YOU WILL COME TO BELIEVE IT IS NORMAL. BEING YOUNG IS WONDERFUL. BEING YOUNG AND FOOLISH HAS CONSEQUENCES.

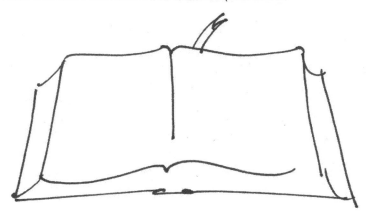

More than anything you guard,

protect your mind, for life flows from it.

—Proverbs 4:23

SCHOOL IS A LOT OF WORK, TESTS, AND HOMEWORK. MAKE SURE YOU TAKE SOME TIME FOR YOURSELF. HOW CAN YOU COME BEFORE THE LORD WITH SHOUTS OF JOY IF YOU HAVEN'T HAD TIME TO BE JOYFUL? GOD WANTS YOU TO TAKE TIME FOR YOURSELF.

Shout triumphantly to the LORD,

all the earth!

Serve the LORD with celebration!

Come before him with shouts of joy!

—Psalm 100:1-2

117

HAVE YOU EVER WALKED DOWN THE CORRIDOR AT SCHOOL AND FOUND YOURSELF JUDGING OTHER PEOPLE BECAUSE THEY WERE DIFFERENT FROM YOU IN THE WAY THEY DRESS? YOU MAY JUDGE A SITUATION BECAUSE OF THE WAY IT SEEMS. GOD SAYS WE SHOULD NOT JUDGE, OR GOD WILL JUDGE US THE SAME WAY WE JUDGE OTHERS.

"Don't judge according to appearances. Judge with right judgment."

—*John 7:24*

DISCRETION MEANS KNOWING WHEN TO BE QUIET, WHEN NOT TO SPEAK OUT OR ACT. MANY STUDENTS LIKE TO BE IN THE "IN CROWD" AND WILL DO OR SAY ALMOST ANYTHING TO BE ACCEPTED. TAKE A MINUTE TO THINK ABOUT THIS VERSE.

Like a gold ring in a pig's nose

is a beautiful woman

who lacks discretion.

—Proverbs 11:22

115

PAUL, WHO WROTE PHILIPPIANS, WAS AN
AMAZING GUY. HE WAS IN A SHIPWRECK, IN
PRISON, BEATEN FOR HIS PASSION FOR JESUS.
YET HE WAS CONTENT IN ANY CIRCUMSTANCE.
HOW DID HE DO IT? EVERY DAY HE LEANED ON
THE POWER OF JESUS. HOW ARE YOU DOING
WITH YOUR CONTENTMENT?

I'm not saying this because I need anything, for I have

learned how to be content in any circumstance.

—*Philippians 4:11*

114

☆ ✶ ✶

AFTER A LONG DAY AT SCHOOL MOST PEOPLE WANT TO JUST SIT BACK AND DO NOTHING. YOU CAN REASON THAT YOU HAVE HAD A LONG DAY (WHICH YOU HAVE!). ONCE YOU GET INTO THAT MODE, IT IS HARD TO GET OUT OF IT. DO WHAT YOU NEED TO GET DONE FIRST AND SAVE THE RELAXING FOR LATER.

The lazy have strong desires

but receive nothing;

the appetite of the diligent

is satisfied.

—Proverbs 13:4

113

EVERYONE LIKES TO HEAR WORDS THAT ARE PLEASANT. TAKE SOME TIME TO USE PLEASANT WORDS TO YOUR PARENTS. IT WILL START THE DAY OFF BETTER FOR BOTH OF YOU!

P leasant words are flowing honey,

sweet to the taste

and healing to the bones.

—*Proverbs 16:24*

GOD LOVES YOU. HE IS READY TO CARRY YOUR BURDEN. IF ANYTHING IS BOTHERING YOU TODAY, TELL HIM. IF NOT, PRAISE HIM FOR THE WONDERFUL THINGS THAT ARE HAPPENING. KNOW THAT GOD IS ALWAYS THERE FOR YOU.

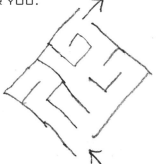

"Come to me, all you who are struggling hard and carrying heavy loads, and I will give you rest. Put on my yoke, and learn from me. I'm gentle and humble. And you will find rest for yourselves."

—*Matthew 11:28-29*

GOD GIVES YOU FRIENDS AND RELATIVES TO HELP YOU IN LIFE, TO HAVE FUN WITH, AND TO SUPPORT YOU IN TIMES OF TROUBLE. BE OPEN AND HONEST TO BUILD A GOOD RELATIONSHIP WITH THEM.

Friends love all the time,

and kinsfolk are born

for times of trouble.

—*Proverbs 17:17*

RIGHT NOW YOU MIGHT BE WISHING TO BE OLDER, TO BE ABLE TO DO THE THINGS YOU CANNOT DO AT THIS POINT. THOSE DAYS WILL COME. RIGHT NOW ENJOY THE DAY YOU HAVE BEEN GIVEN. DON'T LOSE A MINUTE OF LIFE WISHING IT AWAY, FOR THIS MINUTE WILL NEVER RETURN.

Indeed, people shouldn't brood too much over the days of their lives because God gives an answer in their hearts' joy.

—*Ecclesiastes 5:20*

109

YOU ARE MADE IN THE IMAGE OF GOD. YOU
NEED TO TRAIN YOURSELF TO LOOK AT YOUR
GOOD QUALITIES. GOD COULD HAVE MADE YOU
ANY WAY HE WANTED, BUT HE WANTED YOU TO
BE JUST LIKE YOU ARE: SPECIAL.

I give thanks to you

that I was marvelously set apart.

Your works are wonderful—

I know that very well.

—Psalm 139:14

THINK OF SOME KIDS AT SCHOOL WHO LIKE
TO SPOUT OFF WITHOUT THINKING. USUALLY
THE RESULTS THEY GET ARE NOT GOOD. TRY
TO STAY CALM IN ALL SITUATIONS AND TO
THINK BEFORE YOU SPEAK.

The calm words of the wise are better heeded

than the racket caused by a ruler among fools.

—*Ecclesiastes 9:17*

107

ARE YOU HAVING ONE OF THOSE DAYS OR WEEKS WHEN NOTHING SEEMS TO GO RIGHT? REMEMBER TO LIFT UP YOUR CONCERNS TO GOD. HE IS THE GOD OF NEW BEGINNINGS. LOOK FOR THE RAINBOWS IN YOUR DAY, AND THINK OF THEM AS GOD'S PROMISES TO ALWAYS BE WITH US.

"When I bring clouds over the earth and the bow appears in the clouds, I will remember the covenant between me and you and every living being among all the creatures. Floodwaters will never again destroy all creatures."

—Genesis 9:14-15

ISAIAH KNEW HE WAS POWERLESS BY HIMSELF, BUT WITH GOD HE KNEW HE COULD DO WHAT GOD ASKED. WHEN GOD ASKED WHO HE SHOULD SEND, ISAIAH VOLUNTEERED TO GO. WOULD YOU ANSWER THE SAME WAY IF YOU FELT GOD WERE ASKING YOU DO TO SOMETHING?

Then I heard the Lord's voice saying, "Whom should I send, and who will go for us?"

I said, "I'm here; send me."

—Isaiah 6:8

GOD WILL KNOCK AT THE DOOR OF YOUR HEART. WILL YOU LET HIM IN? GOD NEVER FORCES HIMSELF ON ANYBODY; YOU HAVE TO INVITE HIM IN. IT WILL BE THE BEST DECISION YOU EVER MADE.

Nonetheless, the LORD is waiting

to be merciful to you,

and will rise up to show you compassion.

The LORD is a God of justice;

happy are all who wait for him.

—Isaiah 30:18

GOD WANTS YOU TO BE KIND, BE INTENTIONAL IN HELPING OTHERS, AND MAKE A DIFFERENCE IN YOUR LIFE AND THE LIVES OF OTHERS. HOW DO YOU DO ALL THAT WITHOUT GETTING OVERWHELMED? TAKE TIME WITH JESUS EVERY DAY. LET HIM BE THE SOURCE OF YOUR ENERGY.

Those who hope in the LORD

will renew their strength;

they will fly up on wings like eagles;

they will run and not be tired;

they will walk and not be weary.

—Isaiah 40:31

A TEACHER, PARENT, OR BOSS MAY SAY SOMETHING THAT YOU FEEL IS NOT CORRECT. STAY CALM; SAY A PRAYER BEFORE YOU SPEAK. NOT GETTING INTO A WORD BATTLE BUT STAYING CALM WILL EASE THE SITUATION.

If a ruler's temper rises against you, don't leave your post, because calmness alleviates great offenses.

—Ecclesiastes 10:4

WE ALL SIN AND FALL SHORT OF A HOLY GOD.
IT IS IMPORTANT TO TELL GOD YOUR SINS AND
ASK FOR FORGIVENESS. COME CLEAN WITH HIM
AND TRY TO WORK ON NOT REPEATING YOUR
SINS. IF YOU NEED TO ASK SOMEONE FOR
FORGIVENESS, DO SO.

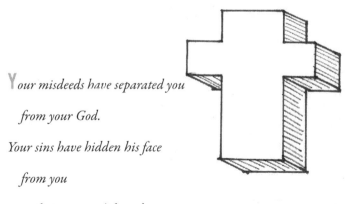

Your misdeeds have separated you

from your God.

Your sins have hidden his face

from you

so that you aren't heard.

—Isaiah 59:2

101

THE LORD HAS DONE GREAT THINGS FOR YOU.
I CHALLENGE YOU TO COME UP WITH AT LEAST TEN THINGS TODAY THAT THE LORD HAS DONE FOR YOU THAT YOU ARE HAPPY WITH. IT IS EASY TO FOCUS ON THE THINGS THAT ARE NOT GOING RIGHT IN YOUR LIFE. CHANGE YOUR FOCUS TODAY!

Our mouths were suddenly filled

with laughter;

our tongues were filled

with joyful shouts.

It was even said, at that time,

among the nations,

"The LORD has done

great things for them!"

—*Psalm 126:2*

AS OF TODAY YOU ONLY HAVE ONE HUNDRED

DAYS LEFT OF SCHOOL. DO A REVIEW OF YOUR YEAR

SO FAR. ARE YOU PLEASED WITH HOW IT IS

PROGRESSING? ARE YOU HAPPY? PSALM 144:15

IS TRUE. IF YOU REALLY KNOW THE LORD, YOU WILL

BE AT PEACE IN ALL CIRCUMSTANCES BECAUSE YOU

KNOW HE HAS A REASON FOR EVERYTHING THAT

HAPPENS. KEEP YOUR EYES ON HIM!

> The people whose God is the LORD
>
> are truly happy!
>
> —Psalm 144:15b

99

KIDS WATCH OTHER KIDS. BE A SPOKESPERSON FOR JESUS. JUST YOUR ACTIONS—SUCH AS NOT SWEARING OR GOSSIPING—MAKE YOU A SPOKESPERSON FOR JESUS.

If you utter what is worthwhile,

not what is worthless,

you will be my spokesman.

They will turn to you,

not you to them!

—*Jeremiah 15:19b*

TAKE COMFORT THAT GOD IS ALWAYS

PRESENT WITH YOU, BUT IF YOU SIN KNOW THAT

HE KNOWS THAT TOO. YOU MAY THINK YOU CAN

HIDE FROM GOD, BUT YOU CANNOT.

The LORD declares, am I a God

who is only nearby and not far off?

Can people hide themselves

in secret places

so I might not see them?

Don't I fill heaven and earth?

—Jeremiah 23:23-24

97

YOU HAVE MANY DECISIONS TO MAKE AS YOU GROW OLDER. LET THESE VERSES BRING YOU PEACE AS YOU MAKE DECISIONS FOR TOMORROW. GOD ONLY WANTS TO GIVE YOU HOPE. SEARCH FOR HIM, AND HE WILL GUIDE YOU THROUGH THESE YEARS FILLED WITH MANY DECISIONS.

I know the plans I have in mind for you, declares the LORD; they are plans for peace, not disaster, to give you a future filled with hope. When you call me and come and pray to me, I will listen to you. When you search for me, yes, search for me with all your heart, you will find me.

—*Jeremiah 29:11-13*

DON'T EVER DOUBT GOD'S LOVE. THE
BIBLE IS FULL OF HIS LOVE FOR *YOU!* GOD
WILL NEVER STOP LOVING YOU. NEVER
DOUBT THAT. REST IN HIS LOVE DAILY.

I have loved you with a love

that lasts forever.

—*Jeremiah 31:3b*

95

CHRISTMAS IS A WONDERFUL SEASON. IT IS A TIME TO CELEBRATE OUR SAVIOR'S BIRTH. THIS CHRISTMAS EVE, RENT THE MOVIE *THE NATIVITY STORY* AND READ THE CHRISTMAS STORY IN THE BIBLE. REMEMBER, THE TRUE REASON FOR CHRISTMAS IS NOT IN THE GIFTS.

The angel said, "Don't be afraid! Look! I bring good news to you—wonderful, joyous news for all people. Your savior is born today in David's city. He is Christ the Lord."

—Luke 2:10-11

YOU ARE YOUNG; TRY NOT TO TAKE TOO
MUCH OF THE WORLD'S BURDENS ON
YOUR SHOULDERS. YOU KNOW A MIGHTY
GOD WHO CAN HANDLE IT FOR YOU. BE
INTENTIONAL ABOUT FINDING THINGS IN
YOUR LIFE TO BE HAPPY ABOUT.

A *joyful heart helps healing,*

but a broken spirit dries up the bones.

—*Proverbs 17:22*

OUR MOUTHS ARE SO SMALL BUT YET CAN DO SO MUCH DAMAGE. IF GOD WERE STANDING RIGHT BESIDE YOU AS YOU SPOKE WITH YOUR FRIEND, PARENT, OR TEACHER, WOULD HE LOOK PLEASED?

Let the words of my mouth

and the meditations of my heart

be pleasing to you,

LORD, my rock and my redeemer.

—Psalm 19:14

92

DECISIONS YOU MAKE TODAY CAN CHANGE
YOUR LIFE TOMORROW. TAKE TIME TO BE WITH
GOD. GOD KNOWS YOUR FUTURE, AND IF YOU LET
HIM HE WILL GUIDE YOU IN THE CORRECT PATH.

How can young people

keep their paths pure?

By guarding them

according to what you've said.

—*Psalm 119:9*

DO YOU KNOW WHAT "EMMANUEL" MEANS?

You will hear it in Christmas carols. "Emmanuel" means "God with us." On Christmas morning so long ago the Son of God was born to be with you!

Look! A virgin will become pregnant and give birth to a son,

And they will call him, Emmanuel.

—Matthew 1:23

90

IN THE PAST YOU MAY HAVE DONE SOMETHING YOU WISH YOU HADN'T. PEOPLE MAY REMEMBER WHAT YOU DID AND JUDGE YOU. BE PATIENT AND KEEP DOING WHAT IS RIGHT. THEY WILL SEE THE NEW FRUITS OF YOUR HEART AND KNOW YOU HAVE CHANGED.

"Produce fruit that shows you have changed your hearts and lives."

—Matthew 3:8

EVERYONE HAS CHOICES TO MAKE. TO BE JOYFUL YOU MAY HAVE TO LAUGH AT YOURSELF WHEN YOU MAKE A MISTAKE, OR ACCEPT CORRECTIVE CRITICISM AND FOLLOW IT. CHOOSE TO BE JOYFUL.

A joyful heart brightens one's face,

but a troubled heart breaks the spirit.

—*Proverbs 15:13*

HOPE IS POWERFUL. IF YOU HAVE HOPE IN GOD, YOU CAN GET THROUGH THE TRIALS OF TODAY. WHEN YOU ARE OVERWORKED AND TENSE, HOPE CAN GIVE YOU ENERGY. YOU CAN FIND THIS HOPE IN GOD.

Do I have anyone else in heaven?

There's nothing on earth I desire

except you.

—*Psalm 73:25*

FRIENDS WILL INFLUENCE YOU FOR GOOD OR BAD. IF FRIENDS GOSSIP, YOU WILL HEAR THE GOSSIP WHETHER YOU WANT TO OR NOT. CHOOSE WISELY WHOM YOU HANG AROUND WITH.

Don't be deceived, bad company corrupts good character.

—1 Corinthians 15:33

LOOK FOR WAYS TO HELP OTHERS WITHOUT LETTING THEM KNOW. IF YOU DO GOOD DEEDS ONLY SO THAT OTHERS WILL KNOW, THEN THAT WILL BE YOUR REWARD. IF YOU DO A GOOD DEED TO HELP ANOTHER AND TELL NO ONE ELSE ABOUT IT, GOD WILL KNOW NONETHELESS. HIS REWARDS ARE ALWAYS BETTER THAN EARTHLY REWARDS.

"Be careful that you don't practice your religion in front of people to draw their attention. If you do, you will have no reward from your Father who is in heaven."

—Matthew 6:1

GOD IS WITH YOU WHEN YOU NEED HIM MOST. HE IS ALWAYS BY YOUR SIDE. WHEN YOU CRY OUT, HE HEARS YOU. EVEN WHEN HE DOESN'T ANSWER IMMEDIATELY, HE WILL ANSWER IN THE RIGHT TIME.

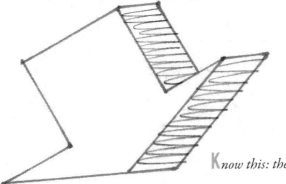

Know this: the LORD takes

personal care of the faithful.

The LORD will hear me

when I cry out to him.

—Psalm 4:3

IT IS SO EASY TO JUDGE SOMEONE WHO IS DIFFERENT FROM YOU, BUT NO ONE LIKES TO BE JUDGED. BE CAREFUL WHAT YOU SAY AND THINK ABOUT OTHERS.

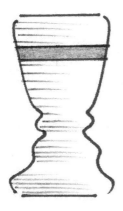

"Don't judge, so that you won't be judged. You'll receive the same judgment you give. Whatever you deal out will be dealt out to you."

—Matthew 7:1-2

YOU MAY HAVE HEARD OF THIS AS THE GOLDEN RULE. GOD WAS THE FIRST ONE TO SAY IT. THERE IS SO MUCH TRUTH IN THIS. TREAT YOUR PARENTS, FRIENDS, SIBLINGS, AND TEACHERS AS YOU WOULD LIKE THEM TO TREAT YOU.

"Therefore, you should treat people in the same way that you want people to treat you; this is the Law and the Prophets."

—*Matthew 7:12*

82

IF JESUS NEEDED TO PRAY, HOW MUCH MORE DO WE? TAKE SOME TIME ALONE AND TELL GOD WHAT IS ON YOUR MIND. JESUS, THE SON OF GOD, ALWAYS TOOK TIME TO BE WITH HIS FATHER.

When he sent them away, he went up onto a mountain by himself to pray. Evening came and he was alone.

—Matthew 14:23

REMEMBER THAT ALL GOOD DEEDS YOU PERFORM NOT ONLY HELP THE PERSON IN NEED, BUT JESUS FEELS THEM TOO. LOOK FOR WAYS TO HELP OTHERS. I AM SURE YOU CAN FIND SOMEONE TO OPEN THE DOOR FOR AT SCHOOL!

"I assure you that when you have done it for one of the least of these brothers and sisters of mine, you have done it for me."

—*Matthew 25:40*

IT IS EASY TO REMEMBER TO PRAY BEFORE YOU ARE GOING TO DEAL WITH A BIG EVENT. TRY TO TRAIN YOURSELF TO PRAY DURING TOUGH SITUATIONS. THE BIBLE THINKS PRAYING IS PRETTY IMPORTANT. DO YOU?

"Stay alert and pray so that you won't give in to temptation. The spirit is eager, but the flesh is weak."

—*Matthew 26:41*

79

WHEN YOU ASK JESUS TO BECOME PART OF YOUR LIFE, HE IS WITH YOU THROUGH THE HOLY SPIRIT EVERY MINUTE OF EVERY DAY. EVEN WHEN YOU DON'T FEEL HIS PRESENCE, HE IS WITH YOU.

"Look, I myself will be with you every day until the end of this present age."

—Matthew 28:20

DO YOU TAKE TIME OUT FOR HIM ON SUNDAYS? THIS ALLOWS YOU TO REST BOTH PHYSICALLY AND SPIRITUALLY. GOD WANTS YOU TO GO TO CHURCH NOT BECAUSE YOU FEEL YOU HAVE TO BUT BECAUSE YOU DESIRE TO.

Then he said, "The Sabbath was created for humans; humans weren't created for the Sabbath." —*Mark 2:27*

TODAY IS A GIFT JUST FOR YOU. SEIZE THIS DAY AND MAKE THE MOST OUT OF IT. START THIS DAY WITH A POSITIVE ATTITUDE AND LOOK FOR GOOD THINGS TO HAPPEN. GIVE YOUR WORRIES AND CARES TO GOD!

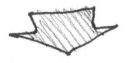

This is the day the LORD acted;

we will rejoice and celebrate in it!

—Psalm 118:24

76

THE WORLD WANTS YOU TO HAVE POWER,

POSSESSIONS, AND POSITION. WHATEVER YOU OWN
IN THIS WORLD CANNOT BE TAKEN INTO THE NEXT.
FOLLOWING JESUS BRINGS YOU ETERNAL LIFE.
ENJOY WHAT GOD HAS GIVEN YOU, BUT ALWAYS
PUT JESUS FIRST.

"All who want to save their lives
will lose them. But all who lose
their lives because of me and
because of the good news will
save them. Why would people
gain the whole world but lose
their lives?"

—*Mark 8:35-36*

75

FAITH IS A DAILY PROCESS OF PUTTING OUR TRUST IN GOD. YOUR FAITH MAY BE STRONGER ON SOME DAYS AND WEAKER ON OTHER DAYS. DON'T GET DISCOURAGED. ASK GOD TO HELP KEEP YOUR FAITH STRONG EVERY DAY!

"I have faith;
help my lack of faith!"

—*Mark 9:24*

ARE YOU DETECTING A MAJOR THEME

IN THE BIBLE? IF YOU CAN BE FAITHFUL
IN PRAYER AND PATIENT IN TIMES OF
TROUBLE, GOD WILL SEE YOU THROUGH
YOUR TRIALS.

Be happy in your hope, stand your ground when
you're in trouble, and devote yourselves to prayer.

—Romans 12:12

THE BIBLE TALKS A LOT ABOUT FAITH. HEBREWS 11:1 GIVES A DESCRIPTION OF FAITH: TO BELIEVE THAT GOD WILL FULFILL HIS PROMISES EVEN THOUGH WE DON'T SEE THE PROMISES COMING TO FULFILLMENT YET—THAT IS FAITH.

Faith is the reality of what we hope for, the proof of what we don't see.

—Hebrews 11:1

72

THERE IS AN EXPERIMENT WHERE YOU SQUEEZE ALL THE TOOTHPASTE OUT OF THE TUBE, THEN TRY TO GET IT ALL BACK IN. IT IS IMPOSSIBLE. THIS IS TO SHOW THAT ONCE WORDS ARE OUT OF YOUR MOUTH YOU CAN'T TAKE THEM BACK. THINK ABOUT WHAT YOU ARE SAYING.

Set a guard over my mouth, LORD;

keep close watch over the door

that is my lips.

—Psalm 141:3

WE ALL THINK WE NEED

ALL THE LATEST
GADGETS—ELECTRONICS,
CARS, PHONES—AND WE
WILL BE HAPPY. GOD
TRULY KNOWS WHAT IS
BEST FOR US. HE WILL
SUPPLY EVERYTHING WE
NEED, NOT WANT.

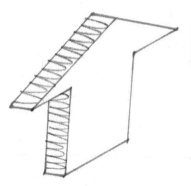

My God will meet your
every need out of his
riches in the glory that is
found in Christ Jesus.

—Philippians 4:19

70

IT IS EASY TO LIKE PEOPLE WHO LIKE US AND TO DO NICE THINGS FOR THEM, BUT IT IS HARDER TO LIKE AND BE NICE TO PEOPLE WHO DISLIKE US. GOD WANTS US TO RESPECT AND SERVE OTHERS NO MATTER WHO THEY ARE.

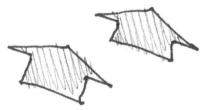

"If you love those who love you, why should you be commended? Even sinners love those who love them. If you do good to those who do good to you, why should you be commended? Even sinners do that." —Luke 6:32-33

JESUS MAKES IT CLEAR THAT IN ORDER TO SPEND ETERNITY WITH GOD YOU HAVE TO ACCEPT JESUS AS YOUR LORD AND SAVIOR. I CAN'T THINK OF ANYONE WHO LOVES OR CARES FOR YOU MORE. IT IS YOUR CHOICE.

Jesus answered, "I am the way, the truth, and the life. No one comes to the Father except through me."

—John 14:6

TODAY IS A DAY TO HAVE FUN, LAUGH, AND BE A LITTLE SILLY. GOD WANTS YOU TO HAVE PEACE. I BELIEVE JESUS WOULD HAVE LAUGHED AND MADE JOKES TOO. ENJOY THIS DAY!

6.8

"Peace I leave with you. My peace I give you. I give to you not as the world gives. Don't be troubled or afraid."

—*John 14:27*

EACH TIME YOU UNDERGO A TRYING SITUATION, IT
HELPS YOU WITH THE NEXT ONE. TO BECOME A
MATURE ADULT YOU HAVE TO LEARN THROUGH EACH
HARDSHIP THAT COMES YOUR WAY. THIS ENDURANCE
WILL FORM YOU FROM A ROCK INTO GOLD. GOD WILL
BE WITH YOU EACH STEP OF THE WAY.

*My brothers and sisters, think of the various tests you
encounter as occasions for joy. After all, you know that
the testing of your faith produces endurance. Let this
endurance complete its work so that you may be fully
mature, complete, and lacking in nothing.*

—*James 1:2-4*

WHEN YOU ARE A BELIEVER, GOD SENDS HIS ANGELS TO PROTECT YOU AND WATCH OVER YOU. THIS SHOULD BRING YOU GREAT COMFORT.

Aren't all the angels ministering spirits who are sent

to serve those who are going to inherit salvation?

—*Hebrews 1:14*

65

FRIENDS ARE VERY IMPORTANT. They understand you and are there for you. Thank God for your friends. If you don't have a good friend at this point, ask God to bring you one.

Two are better than one because they have a good return for their hard work. If either should fall, one can pick up the other. But how miserable are those who fall and don't have a companion to help them up! —Ecclesiastes 4:9-10

THIS VERSE IS EASY TO READ BUT HARD TO DO! IS THERE SOMEONE IN YOUR SCHOOL WHO NEEDS A SMILE FROM YOU? IN THE LUNCHROOM IS THERE SOMEONE WHO IS EATING ALONE? REACH OUT TO SOMEONE WHO NEEDS YOU TODAY.

"This is how everyone will know that you are my disciples, when you love each other." —John 13:35

63

IN TODAY'S SOCIETY NOT LOOKING AT ANYTHING WORTHLESS CAN BE A HARD THING TO DO. TRAIN YOURSELF TO ONLY LOOK AT THINGS THAT WOULD BE PLEASING TO GOD. YOUNG PEOPLE TODAY ARE BOMBARDED WITH MOVIES, MUSIC, ADS, AND SO ON WITH WORTHLESS CONTENT. BE CAREFUL WHAT YOU PUT INTO YOUR HEAD.

I won't set my eyes

on anything worthless.

I hate wrongdoing;

none of that will stick to me.

—Psalm 101:3

ISN'T IT GREAT WE SERVE A GOD WHO FORGIVES
OUR SINS WHEN WE ASK FOR FORGIVENESS? THE
SHEET LISTING OUR SINS IS WIPED CLEAN BY GOD
EACH TIME WE TELL HIM THAT WE ARE SORRY AND
THAT WE WILL TRY NOT TO REPEAT OUR ACTION.

If you kept track of sins, LORD—

my Lord, who would stand a chance?

But forgiveness is with you—

that's why you are honored.

—Psalm 130:3-4

JESUS WILL RETURN TO THIS EARTH. NO ONE KNOWS THE TIME OR DAY. PEOPLE PREDICT THE DATE, BUT GOD SAYS NO ONE WILL KNOW. IT COULD BE DURING YOUR NEXT MATH CLASS OR A HUNDRED YEARS FROM NOW. WILL YOU BE READY WHEN HE COMES?

"This Jesus, who was taken up from you into heaven, will come in the same way that you saw him go into heaven."

—Acts 1:11b

GOD USES ORDINARY PEOPLE TO DO UNBELIEVABLE THINGS. THINK OF DAVID, PAUL, PETER, MARY, AND SO MANY OTHERS IN THE BIBLE. IMAGINE WHAT GOD COULD DO WITH YOU.

The angel said, "Don't be afraid, Mary. God is honoring you. Look! You will conceive and give birth to a son, and you will name him Jesus."

—*Luke 1:30-31*

59

IF YOU HAVE NEVER TRIED TO GIVE SOMETHING TO SOMEONE WITHOUT WANTING SOMETHING BACK, GIVE IT A TRY TODAY! YOU WILL BE AMAZED WHAT A GREAT FEELING IT IS.

"It is more blessed to give than to receive."

—*Acts 20:35b*

IF YOU ARE SEEKING GOD'S WILL IN YOUR LIFE, BE ASSURED THAT GOD WILL WORK OUT ALL THINGS IN YOUR LIFE FOR GOOD. EVEN THOUGH AT SOME POINTS IT MAY NOT LOOK LIKE IT, TRUST HIM.

We know that God works all things together for good for the ones who love God, for those who are called according to his purpose.

—Romans 8:28

57

SOME SINS SEEM MORE SERIOUS THAN OTHERS. TAKING A PENCIL THAT IS NOT YOURS MAY NOT SEEM TO RISE TO THE LEVEL OF STEALING, BUT ALL SINS KEEP US FROM A HOLY GOD. THAT IS WHY WE NEED JESUS.

All have sinned and fall short of God's glory, but all are treated as righteous freely by his grace because of a ransom that was paid by Christ Jesus. —Romans 3:23-24

WE EACH HAVE "SUFFERINGS" WE GO THROUGH AT SCHOOL, WORK, OR HOME. KEEP YOUR EYE ON JESUS. HE WILL GIVE YOU PEACE AND JOY IN THIS LIFE AND BLISS IN ETERNITY.

I believe that the present suffering is nothing compared to the coming glory that is going to be revealed to us.

—*Romans 8:18*

WE CELEBRATE EASTER SUNDAY ON DIFFERENT DATES EACH YEAR, BUT THE MESSAGE NEVER CHANGES. JESUS WAS CRUCIFIED ON THE CROSS AND THREE DAYS LATER ROSE AGAIN TO LIVE IN US! WHAT A GIFT TO CELEBRATE.

"He isn't here, but has been raised. Remember what he told you while he was still in Galilee, that the Human One must be handed over to sinners, be crucified, and on the third day rise again." —Luke 24:6-7

IF EVERYTHING IN YOUR WORLD IS ABOUT YOU,
THEN YOU WILL BE YOUR GOD. YOU WILL LOOK AT
THINGS ONLY AS TO HOW THEY AFFECT YOU.
REMEMBER, YOU SHARE YOUR NEIGHBORHOOD OR
SCHOOL WITH MANY OTHER PEOPLE WHO HAVE
NEEDS TOO!

People who are self-centered aren't able to please God.

—Romans 8:8

STUDY WHO GOD IS AND YOU WILL HAVE PEACE. YOU HAVE TO KNOW WHO GOD IS TO UNDERSTAND AND BELIEVE THAT HE WANTS THE BEST FOR YOU AND WILL HELP YOU IN ALL SITUATIONS.

If God is for us, who is against us?

—Romans 8:31b

52

WHEN PEOPLE HURT YOU, KEEP PRAYING FOR
THEIR SALVATION. IF THEY BELIEVE IN GOD, THEN
THEY SHOULD TREAT YOU BETTER! THAT DOESN'T
MEAN YOU HAVE TO BE WITH THEM, BUT OFFER
THEM UP TO GOD AND THEN IT IS BETWEEN GOD
AND THEM.

B *less people who harass you—bless and don't curse them.*

—Romans 12:14

51

DID A TEACHER EVER GIVE YOU HOMEWORK THAT YOU THOUGHT WAS SILLY, OR DID A BOSS OR PARENT ASK YOU TO DO SOMETHING YOU DIDN'T WANT TO DO? AS YOU PERFORM THE TASK, REMEMBER TO DO IT FOR GOD AND NOT FOR THE PERSON WHO ASSIGNED IT, AND YOUR ATTITUDE SHOULD CHANGE.

Whatever you do, do it from the heart for the Lord and not for people.

—Colossians 3:23

HOLD ONTO THE THOUGHT THAT ONCE YOU ACCEPT JESUS INTO YOUR LIFE, NOTHING CAN SEPARATE YOU FROM HIM. THIS IS THE BEST INSURANCE PLAN YOU CAN HAVE, AND IT DOESN'T COST YOU A CENT!

I'm convinced that nothing can separate us from God's love in Christ Jesus our Lord: not death or life, not angels or rulers, not present things or future things, not powers or height or depth, or any other thing that is created.

—Romans 8:38-39

49

DON'T COMPARE YOURSELF WITH SOMEONE ELSE. LOOK AT THE GIFTS GOD HAS GIVEN YOU AND USE THEM. IF YOU DON'T KNOW WHAT YOUR GIFT IS, TAKE SOME TIME TO PRAY ABOUT IT AND THINK ABOUT WHAT INTERESTS YOU. PURSUE THE INTERESTS GOD HAS GIVEN YOU.

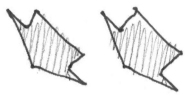

We have different gifts

that are consistent with

God's grace that has been

given to us.

—Romans 12:6

THE TONGUE IS SO SMALL AND YET WORDS CAN DO SO MUCH DAMAGE. TODAY ASK GOD TO HELP YOU USE WORDS THAT WILL ONLY BE HELPFUL TO OTHERS. IF GOD WERE STANDING BEFORE YOU, WHAT WOULD YOU SAY?

Let the words of my mouth

    and the meditations of my heart

    be pleasing to you,

    LORD, my rock and my redeemer.

                    —Psalm 19:14

47

PEOPLE WHO ARE NOT CHRISTIANS MAY NOT UNDERSTAND WHAT YOU BELIEVE IN. BE PATIENT WITH THEM AND PRAY FOR THEM. SHOW BY YOUR ACTIONS WHAT A CHRISTIAN IS.

People who are unspiritual don't accept the things from God's Spirit. They are foolishness to them and can't be understood, because they can only be comprehended in a spiritual way.

—1 Corinthians 2:14

EVERY TALENT YOU HAVE IS A GIFT FROM GOD. IF YOU ARE GOOD AT SPORTS, ACADEMICS, SOCIAL ACTIVITIES, HARD WORK, OR ANYTHING ELSE, IT IS BECAUSE THE LORD GAVE YOU THAT GIFT. GIVE HIM CREDIT!

The one who brags

should brag in the Lord!

—1 Corinthians 1:31b

45

YOUR CHRISTIAN WALK IS ONE THAT WILL
HAVE ITS UPS AND DOWNS, JUST LIKE LIFE.
KNOWING WHAT REALLY MATTERS IN LIFE HELPS
YOU BE ABLE TO GET THROUGH THE TOUGH
TIMES. WHAT PAUL WROTE IN PHILIPPIANS
1:9-10 IS MY PRAYER FOR YOU ALSO.

This is my prayer: that your love might become even
more and more rich with knowledge and all kinds
of insight. I pray this so that you will be able to
decide what really matters and so you will be sincere
and blameless on the day of Christ.

—Philippians 1:9-10

44

TREAT YOUR BODY WELL. Keep it pure for marriage no matter what our culture is saying. Feed your body good foods and exercise. Your body is a gift from God; take good care of it.

O r don't you know that your body is a temple of the Holy Spirit who is in you? Don't you know that you have the Holy Sprit from God, and you don't belong to yourselves? You have been bought and paid for, so honor God with your body.

—1 Corinthians 6:19-20

KNOWLEDGE IS A GIFT FROM GOD. KNOWLEDGE CAN MAKE YOU FEEL SUPERIOR TO OTHERS, BUT REMEMBER THAT THERE IS ALWAYS MORE TO LEARN. STAY HUMBLE—THEN IT IS EASIER FOR GOD TO WORK IN YOU!

If anyone thinks they know something, they don't yet know as much as they should know.

—1 Corinthians 8:2

EACH ONE OF US WORKS SO HARD FINDING THE RIGHT CLOTHES OR HAIR STYLE, BUYING WHATEVER IS IN. HOW MUCH TIME DO WE WORK ON MAKING OUR THOUGHTS AND ACTIONS BEAUTIFUL?

Don't try to make yourselves beautiful on the outside, with stylish hair or by wearing gold jewelry or fine clothes. Instead, make yourselves beautiful on the inside, in your hearts, with the enduring quality of a gentle, peaceful spirit. This type of beauty is very precious in God's eyes.

—1 Peter 3:3-4

41

YOU ARE IMPORTANT IN THE BODY OF CHRIST.

EACH ONE OF US HAS A PART TO PLAY. ONE PART MAY SEEM MORE IMPORTANT TO YOU BUT THAT IS NOT TRUE. THE BODY NEEDS EVEN SMALL PARTS TO WORK CORRECTLY.

Christ is just like the human body—a body is a unit and has many parts; and all the parts of the body are one body, even though there are many.

—1 Corinthians 12:12

40

THIS VERSE CAN BE FOR LOVE OR FRIENDSHIP.

SUBSTITUTE THE WORD "FRIENDSHIP" FOR "LOVE." FRIENDS ARE IMPORTANT, AND IT TAKES WORK TO FOSTER TRUE FRIENDS.

Love is patient, love is kind, it isn't jealous, it doesn't brag, it isn't arrogant, it isn't rude, it doesn't seek its own advantage, it isn't irritable, it doesn't keep a record of complaints, it isn't happy with injustice, but it is happy with the truth.

—*1 Corinthians 13:4-6*

39

IN THIS WORLD IT IS NOT ALWAYS EASY

TO STAND FIRM IN YOUR FAITH. NEVER DENY GOD. WORK DAILY TO BE STRONG IN YOUR FAITH AT SCHOOL, AT HOME, AND WITH YOUR FRIENDS.

Stay awake,

stand firm

in your faith,

be brave,

be strong.

—1 Corinthians 16:13

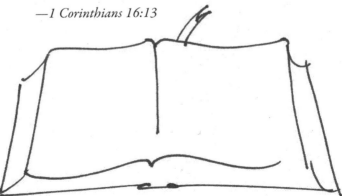

SOMETIMES IT FEELS SO GOOD TO GRUMBLE ABOUT HOMEWORK, TESTS, OR THE STUDENT WHO SAT NEXT TO YOU IN CLASS. GOD TRULY WANTS YOU TO TRY NOT TO GRUMBLE BUT TO HAVE A GOOD ATTITUDE ABOUT WHAT HAPPENS IN YOUR DAY. GIVE IT A TRY.

Do everything without grumbling and arguing so that you may be blameless and pure, innocent children of God surrounded by people who are crooked and corrupt.

—*Philippians 2:14-15*

AS A CHRISTIAN YOU MAY BECOME SELF-RIGHTEOUS, THINKING YOU KNOW ALL THE ANSWERS. IT IS SO EASY TO BECOME JUDGMENTAL. JESUS DIED ON THE CROSS TO FULFILL THE PROPHECY OF THE OLD TESTAMENT. GOD GIVES YOU GRACE BECAUSE OF HIS SON. WE NEED TO ACCEPT THAT GRACE AND GIVE IT TO OTHERS.

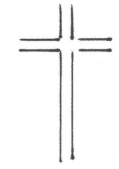

I don't ignore the grace of God, because if we become righteous through the Law, then Christ died for no purpose.

—Galatians 2:21

THINK OF THE MOST SUCCESSFUL

PERSON YOU KNOW, AND REMEMBER THAT
GOD LOVES YOU AS MUCH AS HE LOVES
THAT PERSON. YOU ARE IMPORTANT.

The influential leaders didn't
add anything to what I was
preaching—and whatever they were
makes no difference to me, because
God doesn't show favoritism.

—Galatians 2:6

35

WHENEVER YOU SPEAK TO GOD IN PRAYER, ASK HIM FOR FORGIVENESS OF ANY SINS YOU CAN THINK OF SO THAT HE WILL LISTEN AND YOUR SINS WILL NOT INTERFERE.

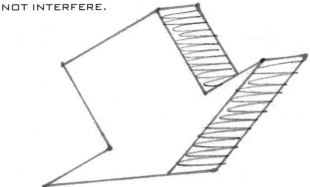

And whenever you stand up to pray, if you have something against anyone, forgive so that your Father in heaven may forgive you your wrongdoings.

—Mark 11:25

BLESSINGS BY PEOPLE WILL PALE IN COMPARISON TO THE BLESSINGS GOD WILL GIVE YOU. TRY YOUR BEST IN EVERY SITUATION. GOD SEES EVERYTHING THAT YOU DO.

Let's not get tired of doing good, because in time we'll have a harvest if we don't give up. So then, let's work for the good of all whenever we have an opportunity, and especially for those in the household of faith.

—*Galatians 6:9-10*

WORKING OUT YOUR PROBLEMS BEFORE YOU GO
TO SLEEP IS HARD, BUT YOU WILL BE GLAD YOU DID.
YOU WILL REST EASIER WHEN IT IS TIME TO GO TO BED.

Don't let the sun set on your anger.

—Ephesians 4:26b

JOY IN LIFE HAS NOTHING TO DO WITH THE GRADE YOU ARE IN AT SCHOOL, YOUR POPULARITY, YOUR MONEY, OR YOUR LOOKS. JOY IS A CHOICE. IT HAS EVERYTHING TO DO WITH YOUR ATTITUDE TOWARD GOD.

You teach me the way of life.

   In your presence

      is total celebration.

Beautiful things are always

   in your right hand.

—*Psalm 16:11*

WHEN YOU EAT BREAKFAST, LUNCH, OR
DINNER, REMEMBER TO THANK JESUS
FOR YOUR FOOD. JESUS RAISED THE
CUP TO HIS LIPS AND ATE BREAD AT THE
LAST SUPPER AND REMEMBERED YOU!

Taste and see

  how good the LORD is!

  The one who takes refuge in him

    is truly happy!

—Psalm 34:8

PEOPLE ARE ALWAYS PREDICTING WHEN JESUS WILL COME BACK. THE BIBLE IS VERY CLEAR THAT NO ONE WILL KNOW THE TIME OR DAY. JUST AS WE WOULD NOT KNOW WHEN A THIEF MIGHT BREAK INTO OUR HOUSE, WE WILL NOT KNOW WHEN JESUS IS COMING. ALWAYS BE READY!

> You know very well that the day of the Lord is going to come like a thief in the night.
>
> —1 Thessalonians 5:2

SCHOOL IS QUICKLY COMING TO A CLOSE.

READ THIS VERSE FROM 1 THESSALONIANS AND TRY IT! LOOK FOR GOOD AND SEIZE THE DAY. YOU WILL ONLY BE GIVEN THIS DAY ONCE.

Rejoice always. Pray continually. Give thanks in every situation because this is God's will for you in Christ Jesus.

—1 Thessalonians 5:16-18

IT IS IMPORTANT TO EXERCISE EACH DAY TO HELP KEEP YOUR BODY HEALTHY. TAKING TIME TO "TRAIN" WITH GOD IS MORE IMPURTANT. IF YOU HAVEN'T STARTED A ROUTINE WITH GOD, START TODAY.

Train yourself for a holy life! While physical training has some value, training in holy living is useful for everything. It has promise for this life now and the life to come.

—1 Timothy 4:7b, 8

IF YOU LACK WILLPOWER OR SELF-CONTROL, OR IF YOU ARE UNABLE TO BE KIND TO OTHERS, PRAY FOR GOD'S GUIDANCE. THESE ARE QUALITIES YOU WILL WANT TO HAVE IN LIFE. THEY WILL SERVE YOU WELL.

God didn't give us a spirit that is timid but one that is powerful, loving, and self-controlled.

—2 Timothy 1:7

YOU ARE PROBABLY FAMILIAR WITH THE RULE OF COUNTING TO 10 BEFORE SPEAKING IN A TENSE SITUATION. IT'S EVEN BETTER IF YOU PRAY FOR 10 SECONDS FOR GUIDANCE. THEN WHEN YOU SPEAK, YOU WILL HAVE HAD A SHORT BREAK TO COOL DOWN AND NOT SAY SOMETHING IN ANGER THAT YOU WOULD REGRET.

Avoid foolish and thoughtless discussions, since you know that they produce conflicts.

—2 Timothy 2:23

25

YOU HAVE GIFTS AND TALENTS THAT GOD GAVE ONLY YOU. TAKE SOME TIME TO THINK ABOUT THEM AND DECIDE HOW TO USE THEM. I KNOW A YOUNG LADY WHO IS A GREAT HUGGER. SHE MAKES ME FEEL SPECIAL EACH TIME SHE HUGS ME. DO YOU HAVE A GREAT SMILE, SENSITIVE HEART, INTELLIGENCE, _____? YOU FILL IN THE BLANK AND USE IT!

In the same way, let your light shine before people, so they can see the good things you do and praise your Father who is in heaven.

—Matthew 5:16

STAY CLOSE TO GOD'S WORD SO YOU
WILL NOT BE DECEIVED. PEOPLE WILL
BELIEVE ALMOST ANYTHING THESE DAYS.
LEARN THE TRUTH FROM THE BIBLE.

> There will come a time when people will not tolerate
> sound teaching. They will collect teachers who say what
> they want to hear because they are self-centered. They
> will turn their back on the truth and turn to myths.
>
> —2 Timothy 4:3-4

DO YOU TRUST GOD ENOUGH TO WAIT PATIENTLY
FOR HIM TO BRING GOOD OUT OF A BAD SITUATION?
TELL HIM WHAT IS GOING ON IN YOUR LIFE. THERE
WILL ALWAYS BE DAYS AT SCHOOL THAT ARE NOT
WHAT YOU EXPECTED. SOMETIMES THE ANSWER IS
ONE YOU HAVE TO WAIT FOR.

*"You planned something bad for me, but God produced
something good from it, in order to save the lives of many
people, just as he's doing today."*

—Genesis 50:20

AUTHORITY CAN BE YOUR PARENTS,
TEACHERS, BOSS, OR OTHERS. ALWAYS
RESPECT AUTHORITY. EVEN IF YOU RIGHTLY
DISAGREE, DO IT IN A RESPECTFUL MANNER.

Every person should place themselves under the authority of the government. There isn't any authority unless it comes from God, and the authorities that are there have been put in place by God.

—*Romans 13:1*

21

THE NEXT SEASON THAT IS QUICKLY COMING IS SUMMER. GOD MAKES EVERY SEASON SPECIAL. ENJOY ALL THAT SUMMER HAS IN STORE FOR YOU.

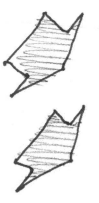

There's a season for everything
and a time for every matter
under the heavens.

—Ecclesiastes 3:1

THE BIBLE TELLS US TO CONFESS OUR SINS TO GOD AND TO THE ONE WE HAVE SINNED AGAINST. TELL GOD FIRST, AND THEN ASK HIM TO GIVE YOU THE WORDS TO ASK FORGIVENESS FROM THE ONE YOU HAVE WRONGED.

But if we confess our sins, he is faithful and just to forgive us our sins and cleanse us from everything we've done wrong.
—1 John 1:9

19

THIS IS A TRUE STATEMENT: IF YOU LOVE MONEY YOU WILL NEVER HAVE ENOUGH. GOD WANTS US TO HAVE MONEY, BUT WE SHOULD NEVER FORGET THAT IT IS A GIFT FROM HIM.

The money lover isn't satisfied with money; neither is the lover of wealth satisfied with income.

—*Ecclesiastes 5:10*

FRIENDSHIP IS A GIFT FROM GOD. IF YOU HAVE A FRIEND WHO IS WILLING TO RISK TELLING YOU, IN LOVE, THAT YOU ARE DOING SOMETHING WRONG, YOU HAVE A TRUE FRIEND.

As iron sharpens iron,

so friends sharpen

each other's faces.

—Proverbs 27:17

THIS WORLD CAN BE VERY FAST PACED. You may need to say no to a few things so you don't feel overburdened in your life. A deer needs just a few things in life for survival—water, food, and safety. Don't fill your world so full that you can't take time with God.

Just like a deer that craves
streams of water,
my whole being craves you, God.

—Psalm 42:1

A MATH TEST CAN BE VERY DIFFICULT. TESTING IN LIFE IS EVEN MORE DIFFICULT. THAT IS WHY YOU NEED TO STUDY AND APPLY THE BIBLE—SO YOU CAN STAND FIRM DURING LIFE'S TESTS.

Those who stand firm during testing are blessed. They are tried and true. They will receive the life God has promised to those who love him as their reward.

—James 1:12

15

YOU MAY SAY THE "RIGHT" THING TO A PERSON
WHILE THINKING THE OPPOSITE IN YOUR HEAD.
REMEMBER, WHAT YOU SAY AND DO MAY BE THE
ONLY WAY OTHER PEOPLE LEARN ABOUT
CHRISTIANITY. SHOW YOUR FRIENDS, TEACHERS,
AND PARENTS WHAT IT IS LIKE TO BE A CHRISTIAN
BY BEING WHO YOU ARE.

Therefore, get rid of
all ill will and all
deceit, pretense, envy,
and slander.

—1 Peter 2:1

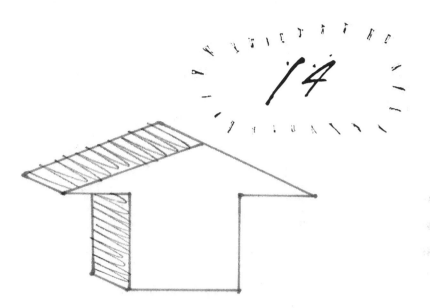

TAKE SOME TIME THIS SUMMER TO GET TO KNOW JESUS BETTER. THEN TAKE TIME TO UNWIND AND HAVE SOME FUN.

By his divine power the Lord has given us everything we need for life and godliness through the knowledge of the one who called us by his own honor and glory.

—2 Peter 1:3

THERE IS NEVER A TIME IN LIFE WHEN IT IS A GOOD IDEA TO LIE. SOME PEOPLE SAY THEY ARE ONLY TELLING A "WHITE LIE," BUT DON'T FOOL YOURSELF. A LIE IS A LIE, AND GOD KNOWS THERE IS NO DIFFERENCE.

A truthful witness doesn't lie,

but a false witness spews lies.

—Proverbs 14:5

EVERY ONCE IN A WHILE WE SHOULD SIT AND
THINK OF ALL OUR BLESSINGS. DOES GOD GIVE
YOU PROTECTION FROM THE RAINS? DO YOU HAVE
A SCHOOL TO ATTEND WHERE YOU CAN PURSUE A
DEGREE THAT WILL ALLOW YOU TO EARN A LIVING
IN THE FUTURE? DO YOU HAVE PEOPLE IN YOUR
LIFE WHO CARE FOR YOU AND STAND BY YOU
THROUGH DIFFICULT TIMES? GOD'S BLESSINGS
COME IN MANY DIFFERENT WAYS. LET'S
REMEMBER TO BE THANKFUL FOR THEM AND PASS
THEM ON TO OTHERS.

*Who am I, LORD God, and of what significance is
my family that you have brought me this far?*

—2 Samuel 7:18b

HOW DO YOU KNOW GOD'S WILL? Read his word, his love letter to you, the Bible. If you have never read the Bible before, be patient with yourself as you learn to unwrap its great truths. Just make sure you have a version you can understand.

This is the confidence that we have in our relationship with God: If we ask for anything in agreement with his will, he listens to us.

—1 John 5:14

THINK OF THE STRENGTH OF A BIG ROCK. GOD CANNOT BE SHAKEN. THE BIBLE SAYS YOU CAN BUILD YOUR HOUSE UPON THE ROCK OF GOD. YOU CAN ALSO BUILD YOUR FUTURE UPON THAT ROCK.

And who is a rock but our God?

—*Psalm 18:31b*

9

KING DAVID PRAYED THIS PRAYER, AND DAVID
HAD WALKED WITH THE LORD FOR A LONG TIME.
BELIEVERS AT ALL LEVELS IN THEIR WALK STILL
NEED TO SEARCH FOR GOD.

Make your ways

known to me,

LORD;

teach me your paths.

—*Psalm 25:4*

SUMMER VACATION IS COMING SOON.

WHEN SCHOOL IS OVER, TAKE SOME TIME
TO READ BOOKS, WATCH A DOCUMENTARY,
TAKE A TRIP TO YOUR GRANDPARENTS'
HOUSE AND LEARN SOMETHING FROM
THEM. NEVER STOP LEARNING.

An understanding heart

seeks knowledge;

but fools feed on folly.

—Proverbs 15:14

LOOK FOR GOD IN THE POWER OF NATURE THIS SUMMER. IF YOU ARE AT THE OCEAN, HEAR HIM IN THE WAVES; IN THE MOUNTAINS, SEE HIM IN THEIR BEAUTY; OR IN A STORM, FEEL HIS POWER.

The LORD's voice is over

the waters;

the glorious God thunders;

the LORD is over

the mighty waters.

—*Psalm 29:3*

6

LEAVE JUDGMENT OF OTHERS TO GOD. HE
NOTICES, AND HE WILL DO WHAT IS RIGHT AT THE
CORRECT TIME.

Don't get upset over evildoers;

    don't be jealous of those

        who do wrong,

    because they will fade fast,

        like grass;

    they will wither

        like green vegetables.

          —Psalm 37:1-2

YOU CAN ALWAYS COUNT ON JESUS, AS HE NEVER CHANGES. THE BIBLE IS CALLED THE LIVING WORD. EACH TIME YOU READ IT, YOU WILL HAVE CHANGED AND MATURED, AND YOU WILL DISCOVER NEW MEANING; BUT JESUS IS ALWAYS THE SAME.

Jesus Christ is the same yesterday, today, and forever!

—Hebrews 13:8

REST IN THE FACT THAT GOD CARES

ABOUT EVERY STEP YOU MAKE IN LIFE'S
JOURNEY. HAVE A SAFE AND WONDERFUL
SUMMER. REMEMBER TO TAKE GOD WITH
YOU THIS SUMMER.

"This is God,

our God, forever and

always!

He is the one who will

lead us

even to the very end."

—*Psalm 48:14*

YOU HAVE ONLY TWO MORE DAYS

LEFT OF SCHOOL. SUMMER VACATION
IS ALMOST HERE. CONGRATULATIONS
ON YOUR YEAR WITH GOD. MAY YOU
FEEL THIS PRAYER:

May the God of hope fill you with all joy and peace in faith so

that you overflow with hope by the power of the Holy Spirit.

—Romans 15:13

ONE MORE DAY OF SCHOOL. LOOK BACK AT
ALL THE GOOD THINGS THIS YEAR HAS BROUGHT
YOU AND THANK GOD FOR THEM.

I will thank you, LORD,

with all my heart;

I will talk about

all your wonderful acts.

—Psalm 9:1

CONGRATULATIONS—YOU DID IT! YOU FINISHED YOUR SCHOOL YEAR AND A YEAR OF VERSES AND MEDITATIONS. WELL DONE! FOLLOWING IS THE LAST LINE IN THE BIBLE. IT IS MY PRAYER FOR YOU AS YOU END THIS SCHOOL YEAR:

The grace of the Lord Jesus be with all.

—Revelation 22:21

SPECIAL FRIENDS AND MEMORIES
FROM THIS YEAR